How To Get Ex Back

Play On The Male Psyche And Win Him Back Using
Techniques Only A Dating Coach Can

(How To Quickly Win Back Your Ex)

Francisco Schwartz

TABLE OF CONTENT

Finding Yourself Again Through The Pain 1

How To Determine Whether A Relationship Is Worth Saving 7

How To Improve Your Relationship 12

Seeking Personal Growth Throughout The No-Contact Period 16

You Cannot Force Him To Love You.............................23

Seducing Your Ex 35

Self-Improvement Objectives 40

Simple Steps To Regaining Self-Esteem, Happiness, And Real Love After A Devastating Breakup 61

Resolving Legacy Problems 96

Find Your Masculine Essence..111

Determine What Went Incorrect................................127

FINDING YOURSELF AGAIN THROUGH THE PAIN

You in agony again? "Yes! It is agonizing and absurd. I must overcome the pain and proceed forward", tell yourself. Every relationship requires sacrifice and dedication. As soon as you realize this, half of your problem is solved. Now is the time to concentrate on the actual process of overcoming the difficult circumstances.

How to Overcome Difficult Times

Many individuals believe that their relationship with their companion or spouse is stagnant and going nowhere. If only their companion would put in a little effort to improve the relationship, it would be much better for both of them. However, their companion either denies the existence of relationship issues or attributes them to the other. In such a circumstance, how can a man or woman assist their relationship?

The belief that it takes two people to enhance a relationship is a common misconception that couples share. It is true that it takes two people to form a relationship, but one person can cause either injury or improvement to a relationship. A single individual having an affair, gambling away the family fortune, or relentlessly criticizing their spouse could cause severe harm. A person who cultivates trust, learns to listen, or spends time with their companion can benefit the world in which they live.

Trying to determine who caused the problems in the first place is another factor that stymies relationships. It is as if they discovered a way to travel back in time and prevent that person from making a blunder. Or maybe it is to cast blame. The first scenario is impossible, and the second scenario is useless.

It is the avoidance of responsibility that prevents individuals from advancing and attaining success in life. What prevents us from changing our life circumstances is telling ourselves that we need more time, more money, more assistance, more health, more chance, etc. People who climb a mountain despite having no legs, start a business despite having no money, earn a degree despite having no leisure, or work on their relationship despite having no assistance experience the greatest success. These individuals are distinguished by their do-or-die attitude and their willingness to accept responsibility. They do not permit any circumstance to prevent them from pursuing their objective. You can be this type of person. You can immediately become the champion of your relationship. To get your relationship back on track, relationship experts suggest the following:

Believe that you can create a healthy relationship by taking the necessary steps despite your partner's resistance. Your actions may influence whether or not your companion engages in healthy behaviors. Do you believe that your current inactivity will encourage you or your companion to engage in healthy behavior?

Stop focusing on who is responsible for the problems. Whether they were your error or someone else's has no bearing on your ability to move forward. Do not waste time trying to convince your peers that you are at fault for your problems. Successful individuals have more skeptics and detractors than supporters. Have the courage to pursue your goals even if others doubt you can succeed.

Focus your attention on the future, not the past. How do you envision your relationship in six months? Five years? In two decades? Do not limit yourself to what you believe you can accomplish. Dare to imagine. This is your existence, and you have the ability to choose how to live it. You can fail to achieve your ambitions, but how far will you advance if you never dream?

Learn the necessary skills to reach your desired destination. People without legs have ascended mountains, but they had to learn how to walk differently and practice on level ground. Get assistance and support from individuals who are motivated to help you achieve your objectives. If you need professional assistance, obtain it. Make efficient use of your time.

Become a person who is deserving of the type of partner and relationship you desire. Do not expect to find Mr. or Mrs.

amazing until you yourself have become amazing. Could you obtain a fantastic job despite your lack of qualifications? How could you hope to find a wonderful partner if you are not a great partner yourself? Are you willing to put forth the effort necessary to attract such a partner? You have done well to reach your current position. To have a better existence and relationship, you must be willing to abandon outdated approaches. To advance further, you must dream new dreams, acquire new talents, and undertake new actions. No one can halt you except yourself.

HOW TO DETERMINE WHETHER A RELATIONSHIP IS WORTH SAVING

Before launching a full-scale campaign to win back your ex, take some time to reflect. Consider closely. Does the relationship merit a fight?

Do you truly want your ex-partner back? Or do you simply feel isolated and insecure? Are you simply concerned that you will miss out on couple-oriented activities?

Do not strive for a relationship that is likely to deteriorate once more. It is preferable to terminate the relationship if the person is likely to make you unhappy again.

You will need to invest time, effort, emotional energy, commitment, and sacrifice if you want your ex back. Does your beau deserve these accolades?

Following will strongly propose that you fight for your ex-partner.

• Your interactions are always enjoyable.

It makes no difference what you do together. Do you share a meaningful, constructive, exciting, or enjoyable activity with him? Or, are you simply lounging around and doing nothing? THAT is something of value if the two of you are having a good time solely because you are together.

• Your ex-partner is one of your favorite individuals.

Do you consider your ex to be a close friend? Do you anticipate looking forward to spending time with him if he was no longer your boyfriend? A affirmative response indicates that you respect your ex-partner as an individual. This is a positive sign for a relationship.

• His presence excites you.

Do you greet and embrace your ex out of obligation? Or do you experience scrumptious heat and agitation just by thinking about him? This is a positive sign if you find yourself physically attracted to your ex.

• You find a great deal to discuss.

Communication is vital to the success of a relationship. It makes no difference how long you have been in the relationship. You should avoid becoming so acquainted with your companion that you run out of topics to discuss. You and your partner should still find it stimulating to discuss your aspirations, dreams, and even seemingly insignificant everyday events.

• You are truthful with one another.

A relationship that is characterized by trust and candor is a wholesome one. No one should feel the need to read the other person's email or text messages. You should be candid with your companion, and he should reciprocate.

• You are capable of overcoming obstacles constructively.

Every relationship will experience difficult periods. How do you interact during such difficult times? Do you frequently indulge in emotional outbursts that serve no purpose? Or are you both inclined to approach issues with maturity and constructiveness?

• You have no strong or profound attraction to anyone else.

Are you intensely attracted to another individual? Is the attraction so intense that you frequently consider forming a romantic relationship with him? Does your ex have a significant attraction to another woman? If this is the case, it may be prudent to end the relationship permanently.

• You have no desire to "pretend" with your ex.

Do you feel compelled to appear to enjoy a particular genre of music, sport, or film? If you believe that your partner will love you more if you act differently, this is not a positive sign. Each partner in a healthy relationship is content being themselves.

• You intend to pursue the same objectives together.

Do you see your companion as part of your future? Does he see you in his? Do you share similar hopes and ambitions? Are you both willing to communicate and reach a compromise if you have different goals? A committed relationship that is healthy is one in which both partners see a future together.

Compare your relationship to the perfect relationship. Does it come close? You should be persuaded that getting your ex back is worth the time, effort, sacrifice, planning, and strategy involved. If this is the case, you should investigate what you can do to rekindle your ex's affection for you.

HOW TO IMPROVE YOUR RELATIONSHIP

It's not just about getting your ex back. You wish for him to STAY in the relationship.

What should you both do to keep your relationship joyful and healthy?

Respect and preserve your uniqueness.

You will desire to spend time together. Couples should appreciate one another's companionship. However, it is essential to acknowledge the need for personal space. Ensure that you do not inhibit one another's individual development. Allow each other time to discover and express your uniqueness.

Nurture trust.

Trust is the bedrock of healthy relationships. The preponderance of relationships with trust issues will inevitably fail. Ensure that you and your companion maintain each other's trust by exerting the necessary effort.

Develop effective communication.

You must be able to express your thoughts to your companion. You are not required to concur on every point. However, you should feel liberated to express your opinions. Each of you should be able to respect the other's position on issues.

Support one another, particularly in times of difficulty.

Finding the ideal partner is not a guarantee of a trouble-free relationship. You will experience difficult circumstances. You will endure hardship and suffering. You will encounter challenges. However, you will have one another to rely on.

Motivate one another to be your "best self."

A healthy relationship is one in which both parties continually encourage and inspire one another to be better and happier people. You motivate one another to achieve your objectives and overcome difficult obstacles. You encourage each other to strive for excellence and not settle for mediocrity.

Be appreciative of the seemingly inconsequential details.

You should teach each other to find beauty in even the smallest of things as a couple. You can recognize and appreciate small instances of happiness. You recognize that these intimate moments are what give life substance.

Be content with who you are.

With the person you adore -- and who loves you in return -- there is no need to pretend to be superior, wiser, or more educated. You are aware that he accepts you as-is. You also accept him as he is, with all of his faults.

Seeking Personal Growth Throughout the No-Contact Period

During the no-contact period, you do not simply do nothing. The purpose of refraining from communicating with your ex for a predetermined period of time is to give each party the necessary time and space to sort out their thoughts and emotions and let negative memories settle. As mentioned in the previous chapter, you are also doing this to avoid giving the impression that you are desperate and dependent -- two traits you should avoid at all costs -- and to give your ex the opportunity to miss you.

The objective of this self-imposed no-contact period is to help you become a better, wiser, and more mature person. Therefore, you must actively seek out methods to emerge from this experience as a new and improved version of yourself. You need this sort of positive transformation to complement your efforts to reintegrate with your ex.

During the no-contact period, you can engage in the following activities:

Work out at the gym. There are numerous advantages to an active lifestyle. First, it improves your physical fitness and mental acuity. Devote a portion of your schedule to exercise. At the gym, a fitness instructor can assist you in developing a routine that is highly individualized and tailored to your specific requirements. Otherwise, you can exercise in the convenience of your own residence. Regularly engaging in this activity will provide you with an outlet for transforming your anger, sorrow, and other negative emotions into something more constructive.

Similarly, studies have demonstrated that physical activity boosts confidence and self-esteem. Therefore, if your ego suffered a significant blow after your breakup with your ex, engaging in a vigorous exercise regimen is a good way to recover your self-esteem.

Engage in the activities you are most enthusiastic about and interested in. One can only wallow in sorrow and agony for so long. You will eventually realize that you need a distraction to prevent yourself from plunging deeper into despair. The most effective method is to recall activities that you enjoy. Consider what makes you the most enthusiastic. Whether it's participating in your favorite sport or volunteering for a charitable organization, find the motivation to do what you enjoy.

- Soak up in culture. Observe performances and films. Visit

institutions. Visit galleries. Attend performances. Never allow your mind and imagination to become stagnant as a result of your separation with your ex. Rather, use this experience as a chance to immerse yourself in the arts and gain a completely new perspective on things. In addition to enhancing your intellect, immersing yourself in culture and the arts gives you a meaningful experience that increases your sense of purpose and self-awareness.

You should read literature. Relax and get lost in the worlds your beloved authors have created. Reading, which is a well-known therapeutic activity, is frequently undervalued by those who view it as tedious or mentally taxing. Obviously, these individuals couldn't be more incorrect.

Set out on a road journey. By leaving your comfort zone in pursuit of something new, you automatically expose yourself to new learning opportunities and experiences. In the midst of confusion and a flurry of emotions following a breakup, what could be greater than losing yourself and finding meaning in it? This may be precisely what you need to determine your desires and gain a fresh understanding of the situation. In addition to bringing back new insights and memories from your vacation, you also have a completely different disposition.

• Write. Keep a journal in which you can record your observations. Acknowledging your emotions by putting them into actual words is an effective method for coping with them. You'll be astonished at how much lighter you'll feel after writing down all of your thoughts and emotions, even the ones that trouble you. Indeed, writing is an effective way to come to grips with even the most challenging circumstances.

Feel healthier by adopting a new appearance. After undergoing a type of internal transformation, adopt a new physical appearance. However, you should avoid making too many drastic changes, as these could be interpreted as desperate attempts to attract the attention of your ex. Remember to be subtle with these alterations. For instance, get a new haircut or refresh your wardrobe. A makeover is a healthy way to enhance confidence and an effective way to demonstrate that you have moved on from the past.

Spend time with your family and acquaintances. Having a strong support network is an excellent method to handle the situation. By choosing to spend quality time with your loved ones, you receive some form of reassurance that you are not alone during this trying time.

Indeed, the no-contact period should be utilized as a chance for personal growth and maturation, because if your breakup with your ex has resulted in anything, it should be the opportunity to redeem yourself by becoming a better version of your former self.

You Cannot Force Him To Love You.

Observe, as a man Permit me to be the one to tell you that you cannot force a man to adore you. A man either adores you or does not at the end of the day. Either he desires to be with you, or he does not. Can you now make a man fall in love with you? Of course you can. So, can you make a man feel in love with you again? I'd say so. Contrary to what some women may believe, men do know what they seek in a companion or wife. Keeping in mind that this may differ from man to man, it is safe to say that men know what they want. It is possible for a man to love you but believe he cannot be with you for whatever reason. It is also possible for a man to have dated a woman he never genuinely loved. Who, then, is your ex? Is he someone who you believe loves you regardless of what has transpired between you two, or is he someone who may have never loved you? This is a question you must address yourself. There is a solution to this problem; if you haven't found it yet, you may need to reread this book.

When I say that you cannot force a man to adore you, I mean the following. Just because you desire him does not imply that he desires you. A harsh reality is that sometimes the affection is no longer present or was never present. If this is the case, you have limited options. However, if you follow my advice about being confident and content, his rejection will not prevent you from discovering true love and a meaningful relationship.

To make a man fall in love with you or fall back in love with you, something must exist to begin with. From there, you must determine what he is searching for and truly desires in a woman. Then consider whether you are or are capable of being that woman.If you answered yes to either of these questions, you are well on your way to getting him to fall in love with you for the first time or for the second time.

Last Words

I appreciate your reading my book. I truly believe that the information in this book will help you get your ex-boyfriend back, or at least find a means to get over him so that you can make room for a new, happier man. Like I said earlier in this guidance. If you believe that your ex-boyfriend genuinely makes you joyful, then use the information in this book to win him back. Remember that it may take some time to win him back, but if there was ever true love between you, there is always a possibility for a reconciliation. I want you to pay close attention to what I just said is the best method to get your ex back. That is to become self-assured and content with your existence. Please do not squander your time pouting and pondering how to proceed without him. Realize that he is the one who is missing out, not you. Stay optimistic and trust that if something is meant to be, it will be. And if it's not you, then another candidate is in the works. Stay Upbeat and Strong!!

How to Get Your Ex Back in Five Certain Steps

There is no need for alarm because there are numerous effective methods to win back your ex. Simply follow these five steps, and you will be astonished by the results. First, let go of the possibility that he has moved on with his life. You should be pleased that your ex is no longer attracted to you, so you can stop fretting about his feelings and move on with your life.

The No Contact Rule: Stop Communicating with Him

Using the no-contact rule to set yourself up for failure requires a great deal of effort. You must have the fortitude to resist temptations and redirect your thoughts. By separating yourself from your ex, you give yourself time to recover. Do not initiate text communications or phone calls. Instead, use your leisure time to socialize and pursue your interests. Ultimately, you must demonstrate to your ex that your existence is significantly more important than your former relationship.

The No-Contact Rule stipulates that you must wait at least six months after a breakup before rekindling a relationship. This is a conservative estimate based on what some individuals say works; the average is between 6 and 8 months. However, the effectiveness of the No-Contact Rule cannot be guaranteed. If you are uncertain, consider what you initially desired from the relationship.

The No-Contact Rule can be useful in numerous circumstances. The most prevalent issue with no-contact laws is that they encourage the revival of old emotions. This can result in heartache and even addiction. You may initially feel lonely and angry, but these emotions will eventually subside and dissipate. Additionally, you will discover your inner fortitude and self-esteem. If you are able to adhere to the no-contact rule, you will be empowered and assured. Your ex will be less likely to reach out to you.

If a breakup is imminent, the No-Contact Rule can assist you in severing ties with your former. If you have already decided to end your relationship, you may not have told your partner. It may appear easier to reconnect after a divorce, but it's not. Whether or not you communicated your intentions, your ex will likely have a different opinion.

In some instances, the no-contact rule is completely ineffective. However, it can be an effective method for regaining your ex's affections. The best way to approach this situation is not to chase your ex away, but rather to delay further communication until he has gotten over the separation. The optimal strategy for regaining your ex's affections is a combination of both approaches.

The Deadly Errors And Ignoring Your Instincts

Instincts are potent forces within the human body that cause constant adaptation and change in response to the environment. They are not intended to drive your ex away. They are intended to ensure your survival by altering your free will. To get your ex back, you must disregard your instincts and create failsafe relationship software.

Get Stronger While He Gets Weaker

The first step in attempting to get your ex back is to determine why he broke up with you in the first place. Women do not always tell males what they want and what will sway their opinion. Instead, they reveal the truth, which can be quite detrimental. To convince him of the truth, you will need to make some adjustments.

First, avoid being irritating, dependent, or obsessive. These three characteristics will make it more difficult to reconcile with your ex, and they will only make matters worse. The Ex Factor Guide describes in great detail how to stop being reliant and begin acting more independently. Additionally, it will prevent you from becoming physically or verbally abusive towards him and his family, which will only exacerbate the situation.

What To Do When He Extends His Hand

If you desperately want to reunite with your ex, the most effective strategy is to be patient and resilient. The Ex Factor Guide can provide the knowledge you need to demonstrate your enhanced ability to make your ex content. This guide is full of helpful advice on how to win back your ex, including how to use your shared history to make your ex feel at ease again. Whether you've been companions for years or only a few months, you'll need to be patient and resilient.

If your ex-partner ditched you for a more fulfilling career or a new interest, it is likely that you have neglected your relationship. Unless you were initially extremely unfaithful, you probably did not give your ex the attention and care he or she required. To win your ex back, you must determine why he or she lost trust in you in the first instance.

The second most crucial step is to determine whether or not your ex still cares about you. This is possible by inquiring mutual acquaintances. You can even ask your own peers for guidance. Step 2 may be the most difficult, but it is also the most important, as it requires you to give your ex space. However, it will be worth it in the end. Your ex will likely become envious and desire you more. You must determine if your ex still has feelings for you if they are interested in you.

If your ex is still lonely after a separation, you must have the strength to accept that he or she will meet another woman and have a child. If you've become acquaintances with your ex, you should consider other options, but not out of desperation. You must be ready for this potential outcome. You might be surprised by what your ex says upon seeing your peers.

Spending time with other people is another method for provoking your ex's envy. It is crucial that you spend time with other people if you're attempting to get back with your ex. This will make them want to be with you more, and it may even lead to attraction. Your relationship could be compromised if you are not vigilant. By spending time with other people, you can make your ex feel envious and allure him or her.

Seducing Your Ex

Okay, so now that you've reunited with your ex and after you've been on a few more dates and exchanged a few more texts, it's time to seduce him and SHOW him what he's been missing while you've been away.

If you want to do this successfully, you will need to acquire the scientific process of seduction outlined below. And since you have complete control over this, the steps below will be of great assistance.

Okay, let's get into suggestion #1...

1.) You'll need to get in touch with your ex and request a private meeting spot.

It must be something intimate, such as a walk through a scenic area or a visit to a cozy coffee shop. Somewhere the two of you can truly communicate. Say that you need to ask them something (for instance, if you're renovating your home, say that you're considering remodeling your restroom and would like their opinion before you begin). Essentially, if there is a compelling reason, they will consent to meet.

2.) If you want to seduce your ex, you must look your absolute finest!

Make sure you appear good and smell good; if possible, put on a perfume that they like. Spend some additional time on your appearance, but here's the secret. Have you ever gone shopping with that individual? Do you recall what you purchased on that day? Consequently, wear that. Or, even better, don an item of clothing that has significance to your ex. Perhaps you and your partner once spent a romantic evening at the shore; wear something from that evening.

Just be sure to wear something that evokes a strong emotional response from your ex. This is what I refer to as photographic seduction, and it is an extremely effective technique.

3.) Discuss how wonderful you've been and how well you're doing currently.

However, do not brag. If you lack the ability to execute this without appearing pretentious, you should not use it; it will misfire. But you want your ex to believe that you have your life together. You might state something like...

"Everything has been terrific! But I've been completely consumed by professional obligations... I was recently promoted at work, and my boss is keeping me extremely occupied."

Or...

"I've been traveling extensively recently! I traveled to Denmark in July 2013. It is truly one of the best locations I have ever visited! Have you traveled recently?

What do you mean? You are implying indirectly and subtly that your existence is awesome.

Now, if you truly want to seduce your ex, you're going to have to touch him or her!

It is not difficult to seduce your ex, particularly if you know what he likes...This is arguably the most crucial aspect of seducing your ex! Yes, I cannot emphasize this fact enough because contact is essential for seduction. Some of you may be familiar with the term "kinesthetic attraction" or "kino." However, intercourse cannot occur without physical contact. Once you master the art of how and when to contact a person, seducing your ex will become much simpler.

SELF-IMPROVEMENT OBJECTIVES

While allowing you and your ex-girlfriend space to process what transpired in your relationship, you should take time to enhance your sense of self-worth and engage in activities intended for personal growth. You do this for two reasons: first, you want to continue living your life to the fullest despite your emotional problems, and second, you want your ex-girlfriend to know that you are capable of improvement. In addition, knowing that you are having fun and experiencing new things despite her absence will naturally stimulate her interest in you and your personality, making her desire to rejoin your life. However, that is going ahead of ourselves.

Continuing to pursue your inclinations and interests is crucial. How? Consider caring for yourself first.

Being physically fit increases your confidence and contentment. When you are in peak physical condition, you experience less physical discomfort and are more likely to have a positive self-image. To be in excellent shape, you must be physically active, and to achieve this, you should enroll in a gym and establish a regular workout schedule. Consult with a fitness trainer to develop a workout regimen that is tailored to your requirements and objectives. You must be sufficiently disciplined to adhere to the schedule and exercise routine you have established for yourself.

Increasing faith

On the other hand, you can also attempt fitness on your own terms. Instead of going to the gym, you can exercise in the convenience of your own residence. You may also participate in outdoor activities like jogging and outdoor sports. In addition, watch your diet and avoid hazardous habits like smoking and excessive alcohol consumption. Keeping these things in mind will not only keep you physically fit and svelte, but it will also enhance your sense of accomplishment and provide you with much-needed confidence.

A requirement of personal development is the pursuit of novel experiences. Being complacent and unmotivated will not lead to success. Actively seek out activities that will test your strength and stamina as well as satiate your intellectual curiosity. Don't let a divorce dampen your resolve to expand your global knowledge.

In this regard, do not refuse opportunities to visit new locations. Travel is a self-rewarding activity; it challenges your beliefs and perceptions in order to provide you with a fresh and new perspective on the world. Increase your knowledge and experience by reading books, participating in the visual and performing arts, watching films, learning a new language, and acquiring new skills. These experiences will teach you invaluable lessons on both a professional and a personal level.

Being honest with oneself

Balance your intellectual pursuits with a substantial amount of enjoyment. Be with individuals who uplift you and make you feel good about yourself. Enhance your social life by spending time with your friends, but never forget your limits. Avoid imbibing excessively and drunk dialing your ex. Eliminate drugs and meaningless intercourse with strangers as a top priority. Do not let your pursuit of enjoyment interfere with your efforts to regain your ex-girlfriend's love and affection.

In all of these situations, it is crucial that you remain true to yourself. Do not attempt to be someone you are not. The purpose of this activity is to highlight your strengths and enhance your sense of self-worth. Take note of the qualities that made your ex-girlfriend like you. Never abandon these qualities.

When your ex-girlfriend finds out that you are doing well after the separation and observes that you are, she will want to know why. And this is precisely the type of interest you need to move forward with your strategy, because if she is curious about you, it indicates that she is considering you. As a matter of fact, women are hardwired to find solace and validation in the sight of males who appear distraught after a breakup. If she observes that you are doing well, her prevailing perspective will be challenged, and she will seek clarifications. Reverse psychology is at work, and this will make winning her back relatively simple.

4. Illustrate, Do Not Inform

Thus, you have accepted the role you played in the demise of your relationship. You are aware of your errors. You are gaining a greater understanding of the ways you could have changed and the ways you wish to change.

You have written and sent the contrition without any conditions or expectations. Perhaps you did not receive a response. Maybe you did.

If your ex responds to your letter of contrition, it is tempting to immediately resume contact. It begins with emails, texts, and phone calls, followed by declarations of affection and additional apologies. This is an error. Continue to maintain a light, graceful, and relaxed tone.

"What if my ex sends me clear signals that he wants to resume our relationship?"

If you believe this to be the case, do not act immediately. Wait a day before taking any action. Ask a trusted acquaintance for their opinion; if possible, show them the email or text message. Obtain their confirmation that you are not simply projecting your own desires onto his message.

"What if my ex-partner replied to my apology with an unkind message?"

These are never simple to obtain. Wait a day before responding, then reread the message. Was it truly unkind, or were you just told difficult-to-hear truths?

If it is a truly unkind message, you must determine if it says anything about your former. Is he truly the man you wish to be with?

If his message consists solely of bluntly stating the truth, then take a long breath. Take as many slow, deep breaths as necessary. Then take your time to compose a composed, mature response to the letter. Again, do not get combative.

What if my ex contacted me after I sent the contrition, but it appears he only wants to be friends?

Or, "What if my ex did not communicate with me at all?"

The ultimate answer to these questions is identical, and the next phase in the program is to implement this answer. Show, rather than explain.

You have enumerated the changes you should have made in your lists and letter of apology. Now is the time to begin implementing these modifications.

Continue devoting time and effort to activities that are vital to you. This is a change in lifestyle that should endure beyond the formal conclusion of the program.

But now is the time to begin focusing on legitimately altering undesirable habits and behaviors. Set yourself a weekly challenge. Maintain your exercise regimen. Make an effort to deflect unkind remarks. Attempt to deliver compliments with grace. Each week or every two weeks, you can add a new obstacle.

Remember that, according to scientific evidence, it takes at least one month to supplant a bad habit with a good one.

It will be difficult. Some days you may feel like you are going backwards. On such days, review your inventories. Concentrate on everything you have begun to alter. You deserve a slap on the back. Most individuals never recognize their own faults. You are exerting great effort to better yourself.

Remember that this portion of the program is dedicated to you. It's about becoming the individual you desire to be. And despite the fact that you are investing in an improved life with your ex, it is a personal development project.

Don't forget about your ex, and don't force him out of your consciousness, but don't let yourself become obsessed with him, either. When you think of him, you should feel warmth and compassion.

And continually place yourself at the center of the program. If necessary, supplant thoughts about what he would think with: "How would my ex-boyfriend feel about the weight I've lost?" With self-reflection; "How does my new, slimmer figure make me feel?"

If it is difficult not to think about the adjustments you've made in relation to your ex, you could try channeling these thoughts into the next segment of our program.

Activity 4: Favorite things of my ex.

Create a list of the qualities your ex admired the most.

Your considerate thank-you notes.

A specific method of styling hair.

Your devotion for certain causes.

How you devoted yourself to an activity you enjoyed.

Do you also like those qualities about yourself? Are you able to invest in them and elevate their status in your life?

Communicating alterations

The term 'show' does not imply 'showing off'. Don't call your ex to tell him that men are asking you out. Don't go to absurd lengths to show off the adjustments you've made. They should begin to emerge naturally.

But to make progress in getting your ex back permanently, you must place yourself in situations where he can observe your changes.

If you have mutual acquaintances

Now is the time to begin attending social gatherings where he may be present. Ensure that you appear and feel your finest.

If you meet at parties or gatherings, be cordial but not dependent. Don't monopolize his attention; converse with others and pay equal attention to what they say.

Discuss himself and what he's doing with him. Do not dwell on yourself, and particularly do not bring up your previous relationship.

But don't be afraid to discreetly demonstrate the ways in which you have changed. Mention that you enrolled in a course, for example, if you felt unmotivated in the past.

When you see your ex in a public place, you may be overcome with emotion. Perhaps he's flirting with another woman or neglecting you. If you become overwhelmed, excuse yourself to the restroom. Take a deep breath or shed a few tears. Communicate with a supportive companion in person or by telephone. Then, cleanse your face and return to the scene with a grin.

Again,'show' and'show off' are not synonymous. Avoid struggling to attract his attention. Focus on being the improved version of yourself that you are striving for. Attention-seeking strategies, such as kissing another person on purpose in front of him, reveal you to be petty, infantile, and desperate. Not the type of person you wish to be.

Do not attempt to incite his jealousy. If he's so superficial as to be motivated by envy to want you back, he's not worth having.

If you do not share common acquaintances

Or, if you believe he is avoiding you at social gatherings, you can take the initiative.

Observe events that you believe may be of interest to him. Exhibits, concerts, and performances. Send him an occasional, but not excessive, email containing a link to an event. Mention that you are considering going and that you believe he may be intrigued. Simply sign off with "Hope you're well." Then, the ball is in his court. You have provided him with an opportunity, which he can pursue at his own pace.

The objective is to maintain contact with him in a relaxed social setting. You must get to know each other as friends all over again.

Remember that you are not rekindling an old friendship. You hope to initiate a new, superior one. Therefore, handle him with the courtesy and restraint you would an esteemed acquaintance.

Taking the word 'play' out of 'playing hard to get'

At this point, a number of how-to guides for regaining your ex's affections recommend that you begin to act manipulatively. They recommend that you occasionally ignore his phone calls or make excuses for not being able to meet up with him. These notions are founded on the antiquated concept of playing hard to get. There is a kernel of truth within the line. You don't want to perpetually throw yourself at his feet or go out of your way to make yourself available to him.

But you are a mature adult. It is unnecessary to perform. Manipulation does not build strong relationships.

If you have successfully completed the previous phases of this program, you should not need to "play hard to get." Your existence will inevitably become richer. You will develop additional pursuits, hobbies, and interests, which you continue to cultivate.

Consequently, there will be instances when you cannot attend a scheduled meeting or a party where you believe he will be. You will be occupied with something else: something else that is important to you. A rendezvous with a companion. A concert.

NEVER cancel something else of equal or greater importance in order to see him. This is vitally important.

Realistically assess the level of importance your ex should currently hold in your existence. He should not be your sole concern. He would not wish to be your sole concern. He would be understandably disturbed if he knew you were obsessed with him.

People with complete, enriching lives of their own are physically attractive.

Don't appear to be that individual. Do not pretend to be occupied and fulfilled. Be productive and occupied.

Moreover,'show' does not equate to'show off'. There is no need to showcase your busy schedule or insist that he is not your only priority. Everyone will be able to tell if you have invested adequately and wholeheartedly in your other needs and interests.

"But I've followed your instructions to the letter. I have been composed and respectful, and I have taken my time. And he still refuses to see me or make communication with me!'

It is excruciatingly agonizing when despite your best efforts, someone does not respond. They disregard your calm, courteous emails and meticulously spaced invitations.

You are screaming on the inside, "Can't you see how much I adore you? Can't you see how drastically I've evolved?

And it is alluring to say them out loud. To exert greater effort; to contact him more frequently; with a greater sense of urgency.

This is the worst possible action to take.

If he does not want contact, he is requesting that you give him some space. He may have valid motives. Possibly, he is suffering from the separation. He may be aware that he requires time.

Therefore, respect what he is saying. Back up. Contact him, but do so less frequently and in a less formal manner.

Recognize that bringing him back will be a lengthy endeavor. We're discussing months. We may be talking about years.

Try not to feel resentful and furious towards your ex. These emotions will only harm your relationship with him.

Carry on living your life. Keep meeting people and making new acquaintances. Continue to invest in yourself and pursue things that fulfill you.

As time passes, your perspective may shift. You may encounter someone else whom you believe to be your ideal partner. Or, your sentiments toward your ex may naturally diminish. There is no correct way to react. Allow yourself to respond to your intuition by paying attention to them.

Or perhaps your emotions will not diminish at all. Six months later, you may still be convinced that your ex is your soulmate.

You alone will know. You alone are responsible for determining how long to persist.

Obviously, there may be additional complications preventing you from reconciling with your ex. The following chapter will focus on the most prevalent issue. What if your ex has a new partner?

SIMPLE STEPS TO REGAINING SELF-ESTEEM, HAPPINESS, AND REAL LOVE AFTER A DEVASTATING BREAKUP

I couldn't disagree more!

After what I consider to be the most difficult heartbreak of my life, it took me several months to begin mending my shattered heart.

Even though I was the one who instigated the breakup, I consider it to be the "toughest" relationship breakup I've ever experienced.

Plus the reality that I detested jumping from one relationship to the next (and still do). Consequently, I desired the relationship to succeed by every wholesome means possible, but it did not.

Though Initially, I believed we would spend our entire lives together, but the love gods had other plans.

After grieving in healthy and unhealthy ways, I realized I had two options: I could remain mired in my misery or I could pick myself up, shake off my melancholy, and make a plan to move on.

Now, my friend, it is time for you to move on and discover new love.

Believe me, there comes a time after every breakup when you must cease crying and begin to consider dating again.

We live in a culture that encourages us to "pull ourselves up by our bootstraps" and "get back on the horse," so to speak, even when it comes to matters of the heart.

However, nothing is more futile than resuming dating or a relationship before you are emotionally prepared.

There are few things worse than experiencing a wounded heart. Not only is it a profoundly sad experience, but there are also a variety of other emotions — anger, regret, bitterness, and in some cases even elation — that can be extremely difficult to distinguish.

But coping with a surplus of emotions is not the only aspect of a breakup that can be perplexing:

Attempting to navigate the dating world after a breakup can be difficult, particularly if you're concerned that it's "too soon."

So, after a divorce, is it possible to begin dating too quickly?

Well, It depends greatly on the length of your relationship and your level of commitment to your companion.

How do you know if you're ready to move on and start dating again after a disastrous breakup?

"The most significant indicator that you're ready to date again is when you've (to a large extent) emotionally healed and have the desire to date again.

If you do not recover following a breakup, you will bleed on those who did not cause your pain.

Before returning to the dating scene, it is crucial to check in with yourself and ensure that your heart has sufficiently healed to handle the many ups and downs of dating.

Ensure that you spend sufficient time recuperating and resolving past issues and pain, but not so much time that reentering the dating world feels intimidating.

Brooke Bergman, a relationship and dating coach, said, "It usually indicates you're feeling courageous enough to risk heartbreak. It is typical to feel prepared one day and unprepared the next. I typically advise individuals not to yield to dread. The majority of the time, we must lean into dread instead of allowing it to direct our lives."

After experiencing heartbreak, it's common to be terrified of dating again, as it can feel like you're signing up to be wounded again in the future.

But if you want the reward (of finding love again), you must also be willing to risk being wounded again, despite the difficulty of the path.

I am aware it's not that simple.

I believed my ex was "the one" for years, and the prospect of meeting someone new and compatible after our breakup was horrifying.

After some time, however, I remounted my horse and continued riding. I feared rebuff and rejection, putting myself out there again, playing the "dating game," trusting a new person, and squandering time with individuals with whom I had no connection.

But I gained knowledge...

"Like anything else in life, finding love doesn't have to be scary and complicated if you follow a plan."

You wish to take a vacation, launch your own business, or become debt-free?

Make a strategy!

Do you wish to discover love?

You must also make a plan for this.

If you have no plan, you will continue meandering around in the dark, hoping to stumble upon true love by some miracle.

Listen up if you're making every effort to find love and are sick of the same old patterns leading you into the embrace of the wrong people.

Give up your ex

Have you truly moved past your separation and forgiven your ex?

If you haven't, you will never discover true love.

On their first date, many people either talk about their ex or can't hear the other person because they're too occupied mentally comparing them to their ex.

This violates the sacred rules of the first engagement.

I am aware of how challenging it is to conceal your emotions. However, the fact that you are still regretful about it demonstrates that you are not yet over the breakup.

According to experts, there is no definitive method to determine how long you should wait after a breakup.

"The only way to know is to be honest with yourself about how you feel about your ex," says certified life coach Kali Rogers.

How over them exactly are you?

"It is safe to date if you are one hundred percent, or even seventy-five percent, over them. Do not date if you are not over them, not even halfway over them."

And realize that if your ex and the breakup are constantly on your mind, there is no space for new love to enter.

Do you still have negative emotions regarding your breakup?

Are you harboring wrath, guilt, or resentment?

If you wish to discover a new partner and true love, you must let go of that baggage.

Whether you're getting over a separation that occurred weeks, months, or even years ago, you must let go.

How?

(You may want to review the previous chapter before reading this one.) However, I'll give you a hint here...

Stop avoiding and repressing your negative emotions first.

We avoid coping with our emotions through a variety of means: sex, eating, binge-watching television, alcohol, drugs, and telling others, "Everything's fine," when we're a hot mess.

Instead of avoiding and suppressing your emotions, allow them to circulate through you and become accustomed to the discomfort.

Do not punish yourself for the emotions.

Ask yourself, "Where did this come from?" and "Why is it occurring NOW?"

Curiosity is always preferable to suppression.

Plus, return to the activities you enjoy. In long-term relationships, we typically loose ourselves. Go engage in activities that uplift and bring you pleasure. Join a new gym, enroll in a dance class, or write the book you've been putting off.

And ensure that you have someone who will listen to you without judgment and allow you to express when necessary.

Do you believe you have no one to speak to?

Think deeper.

You may be astonished at how willing people (such as friends and family) are to assist and listen when you express your pain. It is always simpler to leave no stone unturned when we have someone who listens instead of repeating useless platitudes such as "time will heal."

Community support groups, online forums, and beginning a journaling practice are additional strategies or solutions for investigating your emotions.

You'll be surprised at how much simpler it becomes to let go once you release the burdens.

Always maintain the belief that you have multiple spiritual mates.

Did you just say, "But Nelson, I've already found my soul mate, and they're gone?"

It's great. Not all is lost yet.

And, contrary to what some pastors may tell you, there is no such thing as having only one spiritual mate on the planet. If you've already located one, congrats! However, wonder what? There are more available!

How do I know for certain?

I do not, in reality. But if you choose to remain stuck in your breakup and mourn the loss of your companion, I can guarantee that you will never find another person who brings out the best in you and makes you feel supported, unique, and desired.

The belief that there is only one soul mate is limiting and disempowering, and limiting beliefs are intended to be overcome.

Even if you have not yet found a partner (or soul mate, or whatever you prefer to call them), this is a vital concept to grasp. If you convince yourself that there is only one soul mate for you, you will place too much burden on each new relationship you enter.

Remember that there are millions and millions of potential soul partners for you. You will not discover them, however, if you lie on the couch watching Netflix, feeling sorry for yourself, or dwelling on the past.

Refuse to date individuals solely because they are diametrically opposed to your ex.

Most individuals fell into this trap...

Don't!

When you experience a devastating and overwhelming breakup, you delude yourself that you will never again date someone like your ex! You exclaim, "That's it! I'm dating someone other than my ex!"

Recognizable, right?

Your ex detested spontaneity and adventure. They were not the sort to be loud, romantic, or charismatic?

You are now seeking an adrenaline-seeking, rock-climbing, possibly world-traveling, or swaggering individual.

Your ex had blonde hair, correct? No more blondes from now on!

Your ex did not enjoy reading, cats, Star Wars, exploring new restaurants, opera, camping, meeting new people, or road trips?

You have the concept.

The issue with this strategy, however, is that it is a knee-jerk reaction.

Instead of considering what you genuinely desire in a relationship, you leap in without reflection.

Dating someone solely because they are unlike your ex is probably doomed to fail.

Take some time to consider the qualities your ex possessed that worked for you and those that did not, and write them down in two separate categories (positive qualities and negative qualities).

Repeat this exercise for each of your former partners. Then, write down your fundamental values.

Clarify your standards and values

"Our values are the guiding lights (lighthouse) in our lives." Myles Munroe remarked.

How can you discover someone who shares your values and meets your standards if you do not know what you value and your standards?

Because if you date someone who does not share your values, the relationship will never work... Accept it from me.

Consider your prior relationships as an example. When you first began courting someone, do you recall discovering something that was incompatible with your values?

Remember how you shrugged it off and said, "It's probably not that important after all. Perhaps I will change, or perhaps they will change."

Can you now recall?

Forward to the time of your separation. I'm sure that some of those old conflicts in values and boundaries surfaced during the divorce, didn't they?

Clarify your values and do not negotiate, diminish, or compromise them for anything or anyone.

Stay true to your values and locate a partner who shares them.

If you are able to accomplish this, you will take a significant step toward discovering love again.

Please never believe that you can influence others. This is a common error; I made it in my first relationship.

And here is one of the lessons I've learned from experience: "Whatever you tolerate is difficult to alter. When you lower your standard to accommodate others, you cannot expect them to uphold it.

While it is beneficial to have a positive outlook, defined values, and standards when dating after a breakup, it is not beneficial to have unrealistic expectations of a partner.

Once you understand this, it will be extremely difficult to encounter time wasters.

Say "no" to relationships that are not worth your (or their) time.

If there is one thing that people dislike saying, it is the word "no."

I'm sure you dislike it as well...

It's challenging to say "no." Because we dislike hurting people's emotions and disappointing them, we often say "yes" when we shouldn't. Then we strike ourselves in the posterior for not having the intestinal fortitude to say "no."

When we delay our "no" responses, we waste both our own and another person's time.

We go on third, fourth, fifth, and sometimes sixth dates with people we're not interested in because we can't bring ourselves to say, "I'm sorry, I'm just not interested." Instead, we prolong the process through dread, indecision, and stress.

How do you say "no" to a person you have no desire to date?

Say something along the lines of, "Ben (or their name), you are such a caring, endearing, and wonderful man (or woman). In addition, I've grown to like you as a person. However, I know what I'm searching for in a partner, and you're not it."

Obviously, you are not required to use these precise words. You must strike a balance between being truthful, compassionate, and loyal to your standards and values. Because, if you're clear on what you want after completing

Step 4, there's no reason to waste time with individuals who aren't compatible with what you're seeking.

Ensure that your response does not make them appear foolish for being interested in you in the first place.

Don't be disrespectful!

What's wrong with stating, "You're not the right partner for me?"

Personally, I'd rather hear that and say farewell than feel assaulted by a laundry list of all the areas in which I fall short and the reasons why we are not a good couple.

If things didn't work out with someone, it doesn't necessarily mean I need to change; it could just mean there's a better match for me out there.

Yes, people may be offended by your candor.

But ultimately, that is their responsibility. I don't say this to be cruel; I say it because people cannot develop if you fib to them, coddle them, and continue to say "yes" when you'd rather say "no."

In addition, your honesty will help you both move forward in a healthier manner.

Enhance yourself.

No matter how many self-improvement books and articles you've read, everyone has blind spots and vulnerabilities.

I realized after my separation that I needed to work on a few things. I contemplated my aversion to commitment. I clarified my fundamental values and standards. I worked on my ability to express my emotions regarding sensitive topics such as money, sex, religion, and expectations.

I read new literature on a variety of topics, including business, psychology, habit formation, communication, leadership, and relationships.

I worked with a mentor and traveled alone. I met new individuals and vulnerablely shared my life experiences with them.

It's difficult to take a long, serious look in the mirror and ask, "Where have I gone wrong?

What can I do to improve myself?"

It's much simpler to point the finger and say "It's your fault!" Not mine!"

But genuine personal development can only occur when we search deeply within ourselves.

When you grow and become a better version of yourself, you will gain confidence, and we all know that confident people are much more likely to attract others and find love.

Improve your bad behaviors as well.

It does not matter why or whose fault it was that your relationship ended in the first place. All that matters is that you reflect on any bad habits you carried into the relationship so you can work on them before dating someone else.

If you had patterns and bad behaviors that contributed to the demise of the relationship, it would be a good idea to address them first so that you do not bring them into your next relationship, which can be unhealthy.

7. Appreciate Being Alone and Single

Often, we hear that being solitary is "bad" and that being in a relationship is "good." However, this mindset can cause you to feel compelled to locate a new partner before you are truly ready.

First, try giving yourself a moment to breathe.

Develop an affection for oneself. Self-love is the most essential affection on the planet.

Why?

People cannot get along with you if you cannot get along with yourself. The most essential relationship in life is not with others, but with oneself."

Allow yourself sufficient time to process the entire breakup and construct a life that feels complete.

"Spend time with friends, enroll in classes or courses, and develop hobbies, and then consider adding a partner as a sort of bonus."If you reach a point where you don't mind being alone and can even enjoy it, it's a positive sign that you're ready (for the right reasons) to start dating again."

And if you wish to date, ensure that you are doing so for the correct reasons.

You have no intention of making your ex envious. You are not attempting to occupy the void caused by the breakup. You are dating because you are eager to move on and meet amazing new people.

As I like to say frequently, "you know you're ready for a relationship when you don't need one."

Singleness is a desirable condition that should not be avoided. Your relationship can only be as strong as your individuality.

"Loneliness signifies interior emptiness, whereas solitude signifies inner fulfillment."

You do not desire emptiness; rather, you seek fulfillment. Utilize your time alone to discover your purpose and vision and to become more attractive.

In addition, you can begin to imagine a different future without your ex.

If you can contemplate the future without feeling as though a large part of you will be absent, this is a positive sign.

Whether it was a family vacation or the next step in your plan to move in together, you have begun to imagine going through these events without your partner.

Part of the bereavement process that follows the end of a relationship is reorienting yourself to a life without your ex (or being alone).

Contrary to prevalent belief, there is no definitive waiting period before starting to date again. Nonetheless, if the separation has left you with a few insecurities, it's a positive sign if you've started to feel better about yourself.

An S/O can temporarily make us feel better about ourselves, but this is typically insufficient to sustain a stable relationship.

It is usually when we break out of the honeymoon phase of a relationship that our insecurities begin to flare up.

My advice is to work on those insecurities while being single (and alone) because they are likely to pop up in your next relationship. Being aware of those insecurities can help you cope with them when they arise.

Employ it!

If you are genuinely prepared and dead serious about meeting someone new, you must actively seek them out.

It drives me crazy when people say something like, "I want to find love, but if it happens it happens. I'm not going to go out looking for it! I'll let the universe do its thing."

You've heard such dumb statement before, haven't you?

Are you kidding me?

Like seriously!

When was the last time you were lounging around doing nothing and something that improved your life occurred to you?

If you want to discover love, you must actively pursue it.

Amazing things begin to occur when we put ourselves out there, leave our comfort zones, and confront our fears and doubts.

Attend social gatherings with new individuals. Find community groups with shared interests. Interact with a stranger on the bus or subway. Try online courting if you're desperate.

I am aware that you fear rejection...

If you want to find love, however, you must go out and meet new individuals. Certainly, not every attempt will be fruitful, but that's not the point.

When wonderful things begin to occur (and they will), you will realize your efforts were worthwhile.

Now, these measures are not about becoming unhealthily obsessed with finding love. If you've followed the aforementioned steps, this shouldn't be a concern, as you should now feel more confident in your complexion.

When you improve your ability to say "no," become clear on your boundaries and values, and work to better yourself, you are ready to find love.

Step 8 is not appropriate if you fear being alone for the rest of your life and are frantic to find a partner regardless of how unsuitable they are.

Repeat Steps 1 through 7 until you are prepared to discover love for the right reasons.

Don't forget...

Finding affection is difficult. This strategy may require some time to master.

When you discover that special someone, however, you will realize that all the failures, rejections, efforts, and struggles were worthwhile.

Real love is a lovely thing. It should not be relegated to the status of a pipe fantasy for the lonely-hearts club.

Everyone should aspire for true love because life is significantly more enjoyable when shared with someone who brings out the best in us.

And if you have not yet found affection, do not give up!

It exists outside. And if you follow this plan, I am confident that you will discover it.

After your first meeting with your ex and your declaration of new love, it is time to demonstrate that you are back and here to stay. So, allow one day to pass (but not too many, lest your ex believe you are toying with him or are reckless and irresponsible). Call your ex after a day has passed, when there may be a lot going on in his or her mind, to gauge the temperature. Here. You are measuring the temperature to ensure or verify that your plan has thus far been successful. So contact him/her immediately. Again, getting up early in the morning is a very strategic move. He or she would be delighted to hear your voice first thing in the morning. This will serve as a declaration that you are there for him or her.

Begin by acknowledging him or her. Typically, when an individual (ex-lover) is pleased to hear from you, you will sense it. The person is joyful, laughs for no apparent cause, and desires a lengthy phone conversation. If this is precisely how your ex behaves when you take the temperature and tease him by saying, "Well, somebody is very happy to hear from me," he will blush and either deny it (in a sweet way) or laugh. This is unquestionably a positive sign, as the temperature is "cool" here; continue with your plan, as it's working perfectly.

If a person is indifferent, it does not necessarily indicate that he or she has decided to reject your proposal to reconcile. It's just that he/she is playing hard to get or has chosen to conceal his/her true feelings for the time being. You must immediately break that. Remember that you must put forth your utmost effort. Say something like, "How well did you sleep the last time I left you?" You see, personal inquiries like that get to the heart of the matter; if that person laughs and asks you "why? ", you can assume he/she had a favorable impression of you that night and has been thinking about you ever since. If this individual takes a while to respond, it indicates that he or she is pondering a response that conceals his or her true feelings. This is also an indication that this individual has been thinking about you since your last encounter.

These are all encouraging signs.

Notate the feedback you will receive:

During your conversation with your ex, it is also crucial that you jot down any pertinent details that you observe. This type of information will give you an idea of what may have changed with your ex or what you can do in the future to better impress him/her.

Positive: When you receive positive feedback, record it and use it to your advantage in the future. This will be a means to continue on the same path and a sign that you are succeeding. Positive feedback can come in the form of a confession, a really pleasant phone conversation with your ex, a phone call the morning after your first appointment, or a new appointment set by your ex (which indicates that he or she is eager to see you again). All of these responses indicate that you've taken care of the essentials and that the rest is occurring as expected.

Negative: You should also take note of any negative feedback you receive. They merely indicate that you need to exert more effort to persuade your ex or that you must overcome his/her resistance.

Some individuals erect shields because they fear being harmed and do not wish to appear weak. Take note and ensure that you overcome these obstacles as soon as feasible. It's possible that your ex is playing hard-to-get and wants you to play along for a while before giving up.

Negative feedback may come in the form of your ex not answering up the phone when you call him/her multiple times (the person is usually faking it), displaying no emotion when you call back, or being the polar opposite of what he/she was at your first appointment (being less enthusiastic). Regardless of the situation, maintain your faith and keep in contact. The best response to this type of feedback is to attempt to alter the atmosphere. Contradict the individual's disposition by imposing a more optimistic outlook. For example, if your ex displays no emotion, you could say, "Well, someone didn't wake up on the right side of the bed this morning" to indicate that you've noticed something is amiss. Then, the other person will have no choice but to justify himself/herself, and perhaps your endeavor to make him/her do so will encourage him/her to be more considerate in the future.

If you are not a large fan of taking notes on observations, now is the time to start, as these notes could help you win back your ex's affection.

Here is how you should translate these observations (on the negative feedback) into action: You should use them as prompts for what you should say to or do for your ex-partner.

If your ex prefers to be called later in the day because he or she is busy, convince yourself, "From now on, I will only call him/her after X o'clock."

If he admits that he didn't feel secure meeting you in a public place, use this as a reminder: From now on, our amorous rendezvous will never take place in a public place.

Doing so will allow you to improve yourself more quickly and possibly avoid making the same errors you did in the past with your ex-partner.

Resolving Legacy Problems

Even after a breakup, you may still have affections for one another. It takes time before the sensation completely disappears. And this time period is crucial because we are emotionally fragile and prone to making poor decisions. The emotional roller coaster we are currently experiencing severely impairs our ability to think clearly.

Do not Beg

Probably the last persons you successfully begged and harassed were your adoring parents, and that was when you were very young. As you grew older, your parents developed immunity to your pleading theatrics, and they were also adept at saying "no." You Will Not Achieve Anything By Begging

You never again considered appealing until the day you broke up with your ex, when you swallowed your pride and begged them to take you back out of pity. Begging is regarded as the demon of reconciliations because it only leads to problems in the future. It is optimal to resign while still ahead.

Your ex-partner will view you as a hapless victim.

In common parlance, pleading is defined as requesting something as a favor or reward, which is a reasonable explanation for why it is one of the worst strategies to get your ex back. Why would you want your spouse to get back together with you as a favor? It would portray you as a pitiful charity case.

If you are successful and your ex-partner decides to accept you back, it will be out of pity or regret for how you made them feel. Both of you will dislike the fact that you feel obligated to be together. In the long term, an unhealthy relationship will make you both feel like victims. A relationship founded on such an unstable foundation is unlikely to endure.

You will always question why your partner re-accepted you.

If your ex gives in to your persistent nagging, you will always wonder if it was out of love for you and an inability to fathom life without you, or out of sorrow and compassion. By dwelling on such negative thoughts and emotions, a person's self-esteem can sustain only so much injury.

If you believe that your ex accepted you back out of sheer remorse and compassion, you will never value or respect them again. It makes sense that you would not experience the same level of attraction and love with your ex, particularly if you believe that he or she does not feel the same way.

You both feel feeble and dominated

Begging is a sign of both your and your ex's vulnerability. First, you are feeble for using this strategy to win back your ex, and second, your ex is weak for accepting your return. Two individuals of equal strength always form a strong bond, never a pair of weaklings.

If the foundation of your relationship is weak, it cannot withstand the measure of time, and if it does crumble, it will be difficult to rebuild. Attempting to make restitution for a third time signifies the end of your relationship.

The Simple Answer

Since it is evident that nagging and pleading will not work to win your ex back in the long run, you must discover a different, more effective strategy. You should initially project confidence by remaining resilient and demonstrating to your ex what they've been missing since the breakup.

Demonstrate that you are mature enough for a new relationship with them and deserving of a second chance. Give your ex some space and assume control by meeting their desires and expectations when they are ready to start anew.

In addition to making you appear more attractive, confident, and powerful, initiative demonstrates that you are in command of your life. Begging is a sign of weakness; by acting in the contrary manner, you remind your ex of the qualities that attracted them to you in the first place. As a result, your relationship will be deeper and more genuine than before.

No matter how much you want them to return, the first step in bringing them back is to avoid all contact with them. Abandon texting. Abandon vocation. Abandon emailing. Do not ask about them or their companions. Just cease.

Now think about who you were before you met your ex. Almost certainly, your life was proceeding smoothly. You would have had your own job, acquaintances, and interests. Bring them back to life and help them flourish as they did prior to meeting your ex. Occasionally, some individuals devote so much attention to a relationship that it negatively impacts other aspects of their lives. Your ex was attracted to the ambitious and self-assured version of you; therefore, you should return to that persona and pursue your goals.

Even though you may not feel like it and your depressed mental state may make you want to remain home and wait for the phone to ring, resist the temptation. A smile and some quality time with loved ones are all that is required. Spend time with individuals who make you feel good about yourself and your actions.

Avoid associating with unfavorable acquaintances and associates who may encourage you to dwell in your sorrow. They will not assist you in obtaining your ex back, so you should avoid them. It is essential to reawaken the positive, independent aspect of yourself that initially attracted your ex.

Your ex will become concerned and question why you haven't called or communicated with them. When this occurs, it does not signify completion, but you will have made progress. Consider that if your ex is concerned about you, it indicates that they still care about you.

The key conclusion is to stop communicating with them and concentrate on your own life. Focus your efforts elsewhere and accomplish something. It will serve as both a distraction and a motivator to increase your productivity and attain your objectives.

Be Secretive

Since the first day of the aftermath, both of you have pondered, "How is my ex-partner doing?"

Throughout the breakup, both of you are attempting to avoid contact with one another. It is a transitional period in which the temperature is allowed to drop to an acceptable level. This is a time when resentment issues are being addressed and mutual animosity is diminishing.

At this time, your communication lines with your ex are temporarily severed so as not to interfere with the "emotional healing" period. In light of this, it is preferable that you remain anonymous for some time and keep your ex uncertain. Always remember that ambiguity equals allure.

Go "Underground"

This can be accomplished by restricting access to your social media accounts, which includes limiting your Facebook wall posts and messages. If you feel compelled to share every aspect of your daily existence, do so in a general sense. Never post anything regarding the breakup, whether explicitly or implicitly. Thus, you can avoid giving yourself away while simultaneously pique your ex's curiosity.

Detecting the Signals

Your ex's inquiry will only increase if you maintain your anonymity for a while. The desire for knowledge compels her to seek out alternative information sources.

Your family and friends may function as a relay system. Your ex will ask how you are doing and if you are attempting to move on. This is true!

In addition, strive not to overwhelm your friends and family with information. Again, provide cryptic answers that are difficult to decipher. Simply respond "Fine" or "I'm doing well" if someone from your small group of close friends queries how you're handling everything.

Such responses are open to interpretation, but your ex is now even more intrigued.

In Motion Emotions

If you still have notions of reconciling with your ex, keep in mind that a breakup is only a passing phase.

You still feel affection and yearn for intimacy, which your ex may attempt to suppress.

However, we cannot rule out the possibility that she is experiencing the same emotional void as you. Your ex may want to satisfy certain concerns.

It is crucial that your ex does not learn how you are feeling during the breakup. Keeping a low profile for so long will give her ample time to reconsider your relationship with her. Understand that as time passes, people begin to focus less on the hurt, wrath, and negative emotions and more on the positive, if you allow for a substantial period of no contact. Women require time to ponder their feelings for you. By remaining reclusive and limiting your online and physical presence, your ex will discover how different life is without you.

There will be times when your ex will miss you dreadfully. The possibility of reconciliation may be just around the corner.

Your damage report

The damage report is the subsequent stage. Clarify and be straightforward! What did you do or say that could have a negative effect on your relationship in the future? Did you commit an act for which you were responsible? Have you betrayed her? If this is the case, she was justified in rejecting you. There is no point in pleading with her; if you truly want her back, you will have to alter and prove yourself to her.

In my experience, 99 percent of the time the man exerts too much pressure on the girl, causing her to lose interest due to his weak, insecure, and needy behavior. The masculine energy is neither submissive nor insecure. It is about intent, motivation, and being goal-oriented, forthright, and confident. Uncertainty and submission are feminine characteristics, and a woman desires for you to be more masculine than she is.

Probably, you did the same thing.

The more you demonstrated your weakness and insecurity, the more your ex will punish you for it. She will test you, and the more mistakes you made, the more difficult and lengthy the examinations will be. However, you will be ready for this. If you cried, begged, blew up her phone, or contacted her acquaintances, the situation will become quite dire, and she will make you pay.

The simple part will be convincing her to reconsider you. The difficult aspect will be achieving a different value than before. This can be compared to grocery purchasing; if you have to choose between multiple products, you make a decision relatively quickly. The remainder of your time will be spent searching for evidence that your decision was correct. It is uncommon to acknowledge a previous error in judgment.

You do not need to be exactly as you were when you first met her; rather, you must be a stronger version of yourself, not a people-pleaser. You must be better than she has ever seen you!

In this stage, you will identify the errors you have made. This includes past and present displays of weakness. Recognize poor behavior and work to improve it in the future. Eliminate your dread of abandonment.

Find Your Masculine Essence

You must re-define your masculinity. Find that warrior within you. Take your pride back, straighten up, and walk tall regardless of the circumstances.

You want your woman to follow you, not the other way around, at any particular time in your relationship.

You are the strong leader and you make the decisions, so it is in her nature to follow you. This remains unchanged. Take a piece of paper and jot down the characteristics you wish to adopt, such as the following:

decisive   direct   honest   extroverted daring risk-taking affable etc.

Whatever you wish to represent, simply list it. From now on, review this list, and implement as many of the character traits as possible into your daily existence. I am aware that you want your ex back, but you must realize that this is not possible. You are pursued by women and have numerous options, so you never pursue a woman.

You are pursuing your goal. You have goals to achieve in life other than being a partner. This is a byproduct of your awesomeness.

She must pursue you and attempt to persuade you that she is the best option for you.

This may sound like something from the Stone Age, but it is a fact. Again, exercise your masculinity. Coach Corey Wayne compares the individual to a mountain using an analogy. The woman is mother nature. Sometimes mother nature will shine on the mountain in all her splendor, while other times she will batter the mountain with rain, hail, and violent gusts. However, the mountain does not move no matter what. It is a man's responsibility to be the mountain, steadfast in his beliefs, decisions, and masculine center. Unwavering regardless of what is hurled at him. This is masculine energy, and feminine women are drawn to masculine energy.

You must adhere to the following guidelines to get the most from it:

Exercise at least three times per week
Consume at least one pound of vegetables per day (preferably green)
Do not overindulge in sexual relations or excessive masturbation
Socialize with new people, improve your social skills
Practice flirting with girls

You must reclaim the things you gave up for your relationship, including your talents and interests. These modest accomplishments will increase your confidence. Numerous studies indicate that women find confidence to be the most attractive quality in males.

Whether you like it or not, physical exercise will have to become part of your daily routine. You will appear youthful, have more vitality, and feel better. In addition to the healthy diet, which should contain at least one pound of vegetables, preferable dark leafy greens, fruit is also beneficial. This will make your epidermis gleam, and you will sleep more soundly and better. After about 30 days, people will begin to observe this.

Engage in social interaction as never before. Go on dates and converse with random individuals you meet. Not only to attractive women or women in general, but to everyone. Practice your social abilities whenever and wherever you can! I suggest perusing Dale Carnegie's "How to Win Friends and Influence People" if you wish to become a great conversationalist.

This generally refers to asking the correct questions, particularly with women. If you attempt to win them over and prove yourself, they will be put off by your neediness and desire for approval.

Give them the opportunity to prove themselves. To gain your interest. There is nothing more off-putting to a woman than when she discovers that you are more interested in her than she is in you.

Another excellent piece of advice is, "Read her actions, not her words!" How often has a woman been asked what she desires in a man, only to end up with a completely different individual? Always focus on a woman's actions rather than her words. Women use their feet to vote. If she is constantly contacting, texting, touching, and desiring to be in your presence, she cannot be attempting to get rid of you.

4. What do real individuals do?

When you reach stage four of the breakup cycle, you will be emotionally vulnerable. You will likely disregard the signals sent by your brain and only heed to your heart. Listening to one's emotions is not at all undesirable. However, you may be jeopardizing your ex's return. You enjoy the notion of being melancholy at this time. You will indulge in depressing musings and romantic ballads. Your mind will be cluttered with negative notions. You are a human being with genuine and natural emotions. It will be impossible to deny. Once you accept sadness, you will continue to do so unless you halt it yourself. You must snap out of it and concentrate on your primary objective: reuniting with your former.

As mortals, we are compelled to commit errors. After a messy breakup, many people make these errors, but you do not want to be one of them.

• Avoid speaking with others; you do not want to erupt with regret one day. Therefore, the best way to calm down after a breakup is to converse with close companions. Your peers will not mock you when you are in a bad mood. You require consolation and indulgence. Your companions will spend the entire night listening to you. They will give you a glass of fine wine as you continue to explain your relationship with them. Furthermore, they will hold your head when you need to vomit, as it is obvious that a depressed person will overindulge in alcohol. Let your emotions out. Share your innermost feelings with your closest acquaintances and relatives. Clearly, you cannot tell your story to each of your acquaintances. Choose the friend in whom you have the most faith. Choose an individual you know will answer your call in the midst of the night. You must let everything out. The negative energy must dissipate so that you can create new recollections!

• Getting extremely drunk: Purchasing a bottle or two of liquor is not a terrible idea. However, imbibing your sorrows away is undoubtedly a solution. Consume this vodka over the course of the week. You need to relax a bit, but you do not require additional regret. Extreme intoxication will cause you to do things you may later regret, such as sending a foolish "I miss you" text to an ex. This is likely not the worst action you can take. You may sleep with someone in order to exact retribution. Nobody knows! Therefore, it is recommended to limit your alcohol consumption. A single or even two alcoholic beverages will not harm you. But 5 to 6 alcoholic beverages will cause you to do things you will regret the next day, so be cautious!

- Texting your ex: many people do this and lose the opportunity to get back together. If you are truly committed to reuniting with your ex-partner, expunge his or her number from your mobile phone. You are not required to be drunk to contact your ex. You could do it while entirely in control of your faculties. But trust me; you do not wish to take that path. What do you anticipate will occur if you contact your ex? Your ex-partner may not respond. First, you will text "I miss you" There will be no response. Desperate, you will send another text message containing the phrase "I want to return." Still no response. You will continue to send a few sentimental, regretful, and romantic texts. When you do not receive a response from your ex, furious texts will take over. You will send messages such as "I hate you" and "Go to hell, I do not need you." But do you fault your ex for ignoring your desperate and needy texts? Why would a sane individual rekindle a relationship with someone so needy? You'll only humiliate yourself and destroy your self-esteem.

• Being friends: even if the two of you have agreed to be friends, this will harm your prospects of reconciliation. After being friend restricted, there is no turning back. Downgrade your relationship from "partner" to "friends" It is a poor option. You will not be able to overcome the painful memories of your breakup if you continue to communicate with or see your ex. Yes, you will feel genuine joy because you will be reunited with the person you adore. But critically consider, will you ever move on?

• Begging your ex to return: Have you not observed many of your peers engaging in this behavior? As a last resort, many people implore their ex-partners to return. As previously stated, you should avoid placing yourself in this situation. You will appear frantic to your ex-partner. Consider a hypothetical situation in which you are trapped in a chamber. There are ten exceedingly attractive and physically fit individuals of the opposite gender awaiting your arrival. You have the option to select anyone. Nine of those ten individuals desire you. They salivate over you. You are currently fulfilling your dream. They are on their knees because they desperately desire you. However, you observe that one individual is standing in the corner and neglecting you. This will immediately grab your attention. Why is the tenth individual not attracted to you? Do you now see my point? If you continue to implore your ex to return, you will only boost his or her ego. In fact, your ex may be anticipating a desperate phone call or text message from you. However, you do not wish to grant your ex-partner this pleasure. You want to exceed their expectations and astonish them with an entirely new you, which will capture their interest.

- Engaging in physical contact with your ex: you are a human being and have physical requirements. However, you must maintain it under control. You could make this error in two ways. First, you may have already had "break-up sex" with your ex, also known as "sex during the breakup." Second, you may cohabit with your ex following the breakup. Many individuals engage in breakup sex, so why shouldn't you? Because from the instant you had sex with your ex, he or she will view you as an object of desire. Anything your spouse says after a breakup is simply an attempt to win you back. Many people confuse "break-up sex" for a sign of reconciliation. Those individuals need a dose of reality. In addition, if you continue to be physically involved with your spouse after a breakup, you will not be able to move on. You must eradicate the negative moments. But having sexual relations with your ex will leave you isolated in a desert. You will not be able to avoid your ex. You will be physically bound to your companion. That is not what you want.

- Stalking your ex: the internet is expansive. It has every feature. There are photos and videos of your ex on the internet. If you are still Facebook friends, you will be aware of your ex's activities. You are able to know what he or she is consuming and even where they are going. Two glasses of wine will likely lead you to your ex's profile page. You will investigate every aspect of his or her existence. You will be perplexed by his or her actions. To avoid such misery, unfriend your ex. Remove your ex from all social media platforms, including Instagram and Twitter.

- Reuniting with a person who is not your soul mate: dealing with a breakup is challenging. Do not return to an ex simply out of fear of being unhappy. If you believe that your ex is the ideal partner for you, you should make every effort to win him or her back. However, if you know that your ex is a bully, you should not risk your future happiness by reuniting with a jerk. Sometimes it is best to release certain individuals.

- Becoming a loner: Everyone prefers solitude when they are depressed. You wish you could huddle up in a corner of your apartment and pout. Probably, you will also envelop yourself in a soft, warm blanket, purchase a large container of chocolate ice cream with dark chocolate chips, and watch a movie. Every breakup and wedding in movies and television shows will make you cry. However, you cannot barricade yourself in your residence. You must obtain some exposure. Visit the nearby park or seashore after leaving the apartment. Do not deny yourself companionship!

Determine What Went Incorrect

There has not been a single week in which I have not heard the phrase, "There is no such thing as forever." I'm not sure if this is true, but the frequency with which I hear it is quite alarming. On TV, from my acquaintances and even from strangers! Or perhaps I am spending too much time with my teenagers these days.

"It's not you, it's me" or "It's just not working out"

Now let me ask you a query. Did your former partner tell you this? Most probably correct?You know in your heart that these justifications are absurd.

These are sugar-coated words designed to avoid confrontation and further discussion.

If you were cheated on, that's a different story, but there's still a rationale behind why you were cheated on. Do not fault yourself! You may believe that you have done something incorrect or hurtful to the person.

Perhaps you did, perhaps you did not; we will never know until you get him or her to open up. But disregard that for the moment. You will lose your opportunity forever if you text while intoxicated and ask what went wrong.

Just continue reading and follow the plan that I will set out for you for the time being.

On the following pages, I will explain why your ex may have left you.

I will explain why men and women end relationships. Men typically abandon a relationship when they believe they do not receive sufficient admiration and respect. For women, leaving is a result of feeling unappreciated.

Why do males end relationships?

There will always be an underlying reason why men choose to abandon a relationship, despite the fact that television would have us believe that men are jerks and leave without explanation. I'll be the first to acknowledge that men sometimes leave relationships without knowing WHY. However, that does not negate the fact that there is still a reason behind it; they simply were unaware of it.

Once they began to perceive that they are no longer REQUIRED, they began to doubt themselves and continued down the rabbit hole of anxiety and loss of self-respect. They will decide to terminate the relationship because they will no longer see the need for two people to coexist in the same space.

Never lose respect

Whether it is the dominant in men or the ego, it is essential for men to be admired.

Since the beginning of civilization, males have been viewed as strong and have been responsible for protecting children and women. When they return from a successful hunting mission with sustenance, the tribe accords them great respect and admiration. Men today require this type of admiration from their colleagues, friends, and partner. If their companion does not provide it, someone else will!

Always make an effort to impress males. Put on your finest attire and flaunt it! He enjoys it even if he does not express this.

Men are generally uninterested in drama. Indeed, they detest it. He will reconsider your relationship if there is an excessive amount of drama. It's not that we don't want deeper conversations with you. In fact, we want you to be open, but excessive openness is a no-no.

Why do women end relationships?

Not being completely appreciated is the primary reason why women leave a relationship.

If you want to maintain your women, you must express your gratitude for everything she does.

The condiments in your supper. How she consistently arrived on schedule. EVERY LITTLE THING. I guarantee that women will never weary of being admired. If you tell her daily how much she means to you, it will be nearly impossible for you to lose her.

Constant conflict...

They claim that constant conflict strengthens a relationship. I consent.

I concur that persistent conflict will destroy a relationship.

Arguments that are persistent tend to reopen old wounds and unearth past errors. If a couple continually argues with one another, it will lead to heated arguments, which have never resulted in a satisfactory resolution.

My recommendation is to avoid it at all costs, but not to the extent of avoiding something that requires a formal conversation.

Your relationship is strengthened by engaging in activities you both enjoy. You can travel and exercise with others. These are the two most effective methods I am aware of for fostering a positive relationship between the two of you.

How To Reunite With Your Former Boyfriend

Your relationship with a particular individual has ended, but you want him back. It is not unheard of for a couple to reconcile after some time apart; therefore, you should not lose hope. Before attempting to reconcile, you should give a great deal of thought to the reasons you broke up, as this may help you make the relationship work the second time around.

Consider why the separation occurred. Examine the factors that contributed to the division as a first step. Consider whether these similar obstacles are likely to cause further relationship issues if you try to reunite, or whether you can overcome them.

It is essential to consider what you could have done to cause the rift. Blaming your ex for everything is not an effective strategy for regaining his affections.

Consider the reasons you want him back. Breakups are never simple, particularly when the relationship was not compatible. For this reason, it is essential to consider your motivations for attempting to reunite with your companion. If you want to reunite because you are miserable, lonely, or don't like being alone, you should reconsider.

You should not be with your ex simply because you mourn him. These sensations will eventually disappear, though it may take some time. If you want to get back together with your ex because you genuinely care for him and can envision a future with him, then go ahead and try to win him back!

If your partner was physically, emotionally, or verbally abusive in any way, you should not attempt a reconciliation. It's natural for you to mourn him, even if you were in an unhealthy relationship, but it's important to remember that you can do better.

Take some time. Because the end of a relationship is typically turbulent, it is prudent to give yourself and your ex some space before attempting to mend fences. You must both be able to get past the initial sadness of the breakup and consider what you want.

This does not imply that you should completely ignore him if you attend the same school or have mutual friends, but you should refrain from calling him or hanging out with him for a short period of time so that you can both recover and compose your thoughts.

If your ex frequently contacts you, tell him you'll give him some time so he doesn't think you don't want anything to do with him. This is especially important if the person you adore is shy or insecure.

He may require some time to realize how much he misses you as well.

Recognize that things may not go as planned. When attempting to win back an ex-boyfriend, you must acknowledge that it may or may not work out. Even if you are successful in reuniting with your ex, the future of your relationship cannot be predicted. Avoid being surprised by a second sorrow by preparing in advance for this eventuality.

Build your self-esteem. Utilize this opportunity to actively engage with yourself and concentrate on appreciating yourself. You will be better prepared for a healthy, long-lasting relationship the higher your self-esteem. If you suffer from depression or anxiety, you should seek treatment from a mental health professional. You may be surprised by the effect therapy has on your self-esteem.
Every day, remind yourself of your abilities and talents. Celebrate every achievement, no matter how small.

Talk to your peers and family members if you're having trouble identifying your skills. Ask them to describe what they believe are your most admirable qualities.

Try to be grateful for everything you possess.

Meditation can help you reduce tension and live more fully in the present moment.

Talk to his friends. If you have common acquaintances or if his peers are willing to speak to you without informing your ex, consider asking them about the likelihood that he or she would want to get back together with you. They are more likely to know whether he has a new companion or is interested in reconciling with you.

This is not failsafe by any stretch of the imagination. Even if he hasn't expressed it to his friends, he may still wish to reconcile with you.

Make initial contact. When you're ready to spend time with your ex again, ask him if he'd like to do something as friends, such as having a drink, attending a sporting event, playing a game you both enjoy, watching a movie, or hanging out at the mall.

Behave as a friend, not as a fiancée.
Do not use this opportunity to beg him to accept you back. Instead, make an effort to have a good time with him and to ensure that he has a great time with you.
If he doesn't bring up your relationship when you first meet, don't bring it up. Otherwise, wait until you've spent time with him multiple times and had the opportunity to make a favorable impression as a friend.

Be the person with whom he fell in love. While spending time with your ex in a platonic capacity, provide him with opportunities to recall all of the things he adores about you. Accentuate the qualities you know he appreciates, such as your sense of humor and sensitivity.
Always be cheerful and cordial when you are with him. You may leave hints along the way that indicate your

continued interest in him. For instance, you might say, "It's great to hang out with you. I sincerely missed our time together."

Even if you don't explicitly mention your past relationship, you can subtly remind him of the good times you shared. If he praised a particular ensemble, you should wear it again. You could also share with him a humorous memory. If you have the opportunity to meet him, do so in a familiar location where you and he used to have fun together.

Demonstrate to him that you've evolved. Take advantage of your time together as companions to demonstrate your efforts to better yourself. For example, if it used to drive him crazy that you were always late, make a point of showing up for your outing a few minutes early.

Have an open discussion. Unfortunately, there is no foolproof method to determine whether your ex-boyfriend wants to reunite with you without asking him. When you feel you've had enough time to show him the new and improved you, have an honest conversation with him, letting him know that you still have feelings for him.

Be sure to ask your ex if he still has feelings for you too before you start gushing about wanting to get back together. There's not much you can do if he doesn't comply.

Do not weep or plead.

Don't turn this conversation into an argument about why the relationship ended. It is essential to demonstrate him that you have moved on from that.

Have the conversation in a place where you will not be interrupted and where it will be peaceful.

Commit to improving your relationships. If your ex-boyfriend accepts you back, you and he must take measures to ensure that the issues that led to your previous breakup do not interfere with your relationship in the future. Discuss the types of conflicts you have experienced in the past and how you could manage them more effectively in the future.

Depending on the seriousness of your relationship with your boyfriend, you may need couples counseling to enhance your relationship skills.

Eliminate bad behaviors. Now is the time to examine your actions that led to the breakup and make an effort to better yourself. If you believe that you and your ex broke up because you were too possessive or argumentative, try being more aware of these tendencies and stopping them in their tracks.

Depending on the undesirable behaviors you wish to eliminate, you may benefit from the assistance of a mental health professional.

Keep in mind that this does not imply that you should alter your identity. If your personalities are incompatible, you should undoubtedly find a new boyfriend who accepts you for who you are. If you have bad behaviors that you can change, however, you should work on them.

You need not alter for anyone else! Any adjustments you make should be made because they will benefit you in the long run.

Apologize if you have caused him harm. If you did anything to harm your ex-boyfriend, such as saying something offensive or not being there for him when he needed you, it's time to apologize. It takes great courage to apologize sincerely, but doing so will go a long way toward repairing your relationship.

Be specific in your expression of regret. Instead of "I'm sorry for hurting you," you should say "I'm sorry for not returning your calls." This will help convince him that you have thoughtfully considered the things for which you must apologize.

Explain to your ex why you did what you did and what you learned from the experience.

Demonstrate your faithfulness. If you and your ex broke up because you were unfaithful, you face the daunting task of convincing him that you will not cheat again. Depending on why you deceived in the first place, you should approach the issue differently, but regardless of the reason, you must be open and honest with him.

If you cheated because you were unhappy in the relationship or felt that something was missing, be honest about what happened and what you would like to do to make sure it doesn't happen again.

If you cheated because you thought you had genuine feelings for the other person but you didn't, let your ex-boyfriend know how wrong you were and tell him what you've learned.

If you are a compulsive cheater and are uncertain of your motivations, demonstrate your dedication by pursuing professional psychiatric counseling.

If you cheated on your ex-boyfriend to exact revenge or teach him a lesson, tell him that you realize how immature your actions were and that you've learned how essential it is to resolve conflicts as an adult.

Focus on long-distance concerns. Don't lose hope if you and your boyfriend broke up because you couldn't make your long-distance relationship work! It is possible to make long-distance relationships work if you maintain your resolve and give your companion the attention he requires.

Commit to regular conversations, and ensure that you are always honest and transparent with your partner. If you are unable to be physically near to him, it is even more crucial to focus on communication.

Share even the most mundane details of your daily existence with your partner and encourage him to do the same. This will help you sense a part of the other person's world.

Try your hardest not to let the distance cause you to feel apprehensive about your relationship, as these doubts could lead to its demise.

Ensure you desire your ex-partner's return for the right reasons. Are you still sincerely in love with him? If this is the case, it may be worthwhile to endeavor to win him back by demonstrating that you still care and that things will be better this time. Sometimes a breakup allows both parties to realize that they want to be together again more than anything else. If you want your ex back for any other reason, you should reconsider whether it's a good idea to try to revive the relationship.

For instance, if you want him back because you're lonely without him, that is not a sufficient reason to reunite. The feeling of isolation will fade with time.

Or, if you want him back because you are envious of him being with someone else, you should consider carefully before attempting to reunite. Envy after a breakup is prevalent, and it too will pass.

Consider attentively if he is in a relationship with someone else. If your ex-lover has started dating someone else, he is off-limits. Don't become that person who won't leave her ex-boyfriend alone after he's moved on. If he is content with someone else, your interference could end up harming him, his new partner, and you.

Stop trying to win back your ex if the relationship was toxic or violent. Following the end of a tumultuous relationship, it may feel lonely or even monotonous to be on your own, but you should resist the urge to return to your ex-partner. On-again, off-again relationships are typically characterized by enduringly deleterious tendencies. Resist the temptation to rush back in when you realize you're better off apart.

Since you are sad, emotionally exhausted, and most of all confused after a divorce, it is crucial to have a plan. And while in this state of confusion, you are likely to make mistakes that will hinder your chances of reuniting and make you feel dreadful.

www.ingramcontent.com/pod-product-compliance
Lightning Source LLC
Chambersburg PA
CBHW050244120526
44590CB00016B/2208